MAKING MONEY ON SOCIAL MEDIA (2024 & BEYOND)

Transform Followers and Likes into Financial

Success

TRACI FISCHER

CONTENTS

INTRODUCTION   **8**

UNDERSTANDING SOCIAL MEDIA PLATFORMS   **14**

1. Instagram   15
      User Demographics: 15
      Unique Features and Opportunities   16

2. YouTube   17
      User Demographics: 17
      Unique Features and Opportunities: 18

3. TikTok   19
      User Demographics: 19
      Unique Features and Opportunities: 20

4. Twitter   21
      User Demographics: 21
      Unique Features and Opportunities: 21

5. LinkedIn   23
      User Demographics: 23
      Unique Features and Opportunities: 23

6. Pinterest   24
      User Demographics: 24
      Unique Features and Opportunities: 25

7. Snapchat   26
      User Demographics: 26
      Unique Features and Opportunities: 26

BUILDING A PERSONAL BRAND   **28**

Importance of a Cohesive Brand Image   29
      Here are some tips for creating a cohesive brand

image: 29

Here's a step-by-step process to help you craft an engaging bio: 31

Strategies for Creating Engaging and Authentic Content 37

MONETIZING CONTENT **41**

1. Sponsored Posts: 41

Pros: 42

Cons: 43

2. Affiliate Marketing: 43

Pros: 44

Cons: 45

3. Selling Products/Services: 45

Pros: 46

Cons: 47

4. Memberships and Subscriptions: 47

Pros: 48

Cons: 49

5. Ad Revenue: 49

Pros: 50

Cons: 51

GROWING YOUR AUDIENCE **53**

Tips for Increasing Followers Organically 54

Consistent and Quality Content: 54

Optimize Profile and Bio: 55

Engage with Your Community: 55

Utilize Hashtags Effectively: 56

Collaborate with Your Followers: 56

Collaborations and Cross-Promotion Strategies 57

Identify Compatible Collaborators: 57

    Cross-Promotion on Multiple Platforms: 58

    Host Giveaways and Contests: 58

    Guest Contributions and Takeovers: 59

    Join Collaborative Campaigns: 59

    Share Each Other's Content: 60

ANALYTICS AND DATA INSIGHTS   **62**

Understanding Audience Behavior through Analytics 63

    Choose the Right Analytics Tools: 63

    Identify Key Metrics: 64

    Track Audience Demographics: 64

    Analyze Content Performance: 65

    Monitor Audience Engagement: 66

Utilizing Data to Optimize Content Strategy and Monetization Efforts   66

    Identify High-Performing Content: 66

    Content Scheduling and Timing: 67

    Content Diversification Strategies: 67

    Evaluate Monetization Strategies: 68

    Optimize Ad Campaigns: 69

    Conversion Tracking: 69

    Iterative Strategy Refinement: 70

LEGAL AND ETHICAL CONSIDERATIONS IN NAVIGATING THE SOCIAL MEDIA LANDSCAPE   **72**

Legal Considerations   73

    Copyright Issues: 73

    Disclosure Requirements: 74

    Privacy Laws: 74

Defamation and Libel: 75
Contest and Giveaway Compliance: 76
Ethical Practices for Maintaining Audience Trust: 76
Authenticity and Transparency: 76
User Consent and Respect: 77
Avoid Deceptive Marketing Practices: 78
Community Engagement: 78
Responsible Influencer Marketing: 79
Avoiding Plagiarism and Proper Attribution: 79
DIVERSIFYING INCOME STREAMS   **82**
Beyond Social Media: Exploring Additional Revenue
Streams   83
Online Courses and Educational Content: 83
Merchandise and E-commerce: 83
Affiliate Marketing Beyond Social Media: 84
Consulting or Coaching Services: 85
Public Speaking Engagements: 85
Writing and Content Creation for Others: 86
Embracing a Diversified Approach for Long-Term
Sustainability   87
Risk Mitigation: 87
Audience Expansion: 87
Adaptability to Market Trends: 88
Resilience in Economic Downturns: 89
Leveraging Existing Skills: 89
Building a Sustainable Brand Ecosystem: 90
**OVERCOMING CHALLENGES IN THE SOCIAL
MEDIA LANDSCAPE**   **92**
Algorithm Changes: 93

Dealing with Negativity: 94
Follower Fluctuations: 95
Content Saturation: 96
Evolving Trends: 97
Privacy Concerns: 98
Platform Dependence: 100
Coping with Burnout: 101
SUCCESS STORIES AND CASE STUDIES   **104**
**FUTURE TRENDS AND ADAPTATION IN SOCIAL
MEDIA**   **114**
Emerging Trends in Social Media   115
   Short-Form Video Dominance   115
   Virtual and Augmented Reality Integration: 115
   Niche Communities and Micro-Influencers   116
   Ephemeral Content and Disappearing Stories 117
   Social Commerce Evolution   117
Staying Ahead of the Curve   118
   Continuous Learning and Skill Development   118
   Experimentation and Risk-Taking   119
   Community Engagement and Feedback   119
   Cross-Platform Presence   120
   Data Analysis and Insights Utilization   121
   Networking and Collaboration   121
   Agility and Adaptability   122
CONCLUSION   **125**

INTRODUCTION

In the ever-evolving landscape of contemporary business, the role of social media has transcended mere connectivity and communication, becoming a powerful catalyst for economic opportunities. As I navigate a digital era characterized by unprecedented connectivity, social media platforms have emerged as dynamic arenas where businesses and individuals alike can thrive, redefine their brand presence, and unlock new streams of income.

The importance of social media in the modern business landscape cannot be overstated. These platforms serve as virtual marketplaces, connecting businesses directly with their target audiences in ways unimaginable just a few years ago. Social media's pervasive reach allows enterprises to transcend geographical boundaries, enabling them to engage with a global audience and establish a digital footprint that extends far beyond traditional marketing channels.

Notably, the potential for individuals to leverage social media for income has become a transformative aspect of this digital revolution. Social media platforms provide a democratized space where anyone with a compelling voice, unique skills, or a distinct perspective can carve out a niche and build a following. The democratization of online presence allows individuals to become creators, entrepreneurs, and influencers, shaping their own economic destinies in the process.

The democratization of online presence allows individuals to become creators, entrepreneurs, and influencers, shaping their own economic destinies in the process.

The rise of influencers, content creators, and digital entrepreneurs exemplifies the transformative power of social media. Platforms like Instagram, YouTube, and TikTok have given birth to a new breed of self-made professionals who harness the potency of their personal brand to generate income streams. Whether through sponsored collaborations, affiliate marketing, or direct sales, individuals can turn their passion and expertise into lucrative ventures, challenging traditional notions of employment and income generation.

This book endeavors to delve into the multifaceted realm of making money on social media, providing insights, strategies, and practical advice for individuals seeking to harness the economic potential inherent in these digital landscapes. From understanding the nuances of various social media platforms to navigating the intricacies of building a personal brand and implementing effective monetization strategies, this guide aims to empower readers to navigate the dynamic world of social media with confidence and financial acumen.

As I embark on this exploration, it is crucial to recognize that social media is not merely a tool for communication but a dynamic marketplace where individuals can shape their destinies, redefine success, and unlock a myriad of possibilities. Join me on this journey as I unravel the intricacies of making money on social media and explore the transformative impact these platforms can have on our professional lives.

UNDERSTANDING SOCIAL MEDIA PLATFORMS

In the expansive landscape of social media, platforms such as Instagram, YouTube, and TikTok stand as pillars, each with its unique characteristics, user demographics, and unparalleled opportunities. To navigate the diverse terrain of these digital spaces, it is imperative to comprehend the nuances of each platform, recognizing the distinct advantages they offer to individuals seeking to leverage them for personal or professional gain.

1. Instagram

Instagram, a visual-centric platform, has evolved into a powerhouse with over a billion active users. It particularly resonates with younger demographics, with a significant user base of individuals aged 18 to 34. The platform's visually-driven nature makes it ideal for content creators, photographers, fashion enthusiasts, and lifestyle influencers seeking to showcase their creativity.

Unique Features and Opportunities

Instagram's ecosystem is characterized by its emphasis on visuals, making it an ideal space for aesthetically pleasing content. Features such as Instagram Stories, IGTV, and Reels offer versatile avenues for engagement. The platform's influencer marketing potential is vast, allowing individuals to collaborate with brands, promote products, and monetize their content through sponsored posts. The visual appeal of Instagram fosters a highly engaged community, making it a potent platform for those who can craft compelling imagery and storytelling.

2. YouTube

YouTube, a video-sharing giant, boasts an expansive user base that spans all age groups. With over 2 billion logged-in monthly users, it caters to a diverse audience seeking content ranging from educational tutorials to entertainment. YouTube's global reach ensures a broad demographic appeal, making it a go-to platform for those with a passion for video content creation.

Unique Features and Opportunities:

YouTube's primary strength lies in its video-centric format, providing content creators with a platform to share longer-form videos. Features like YouTube Live and Premiere enhance real-time engagement with audiences. The platform's monetization options, including ad revenue, channel memberships, and Super Chat, offer diverse income streams for creators. Its search-centric algorithm enables evergreen content to attract views over time, contributing to sustained revenue potential.

3. TikTok

TikTok, a short-form video platform, has rapidly gained popularity, particularly among younger users. With a predominantly Gen Z user base, TikTok has become synonymous with creative, bite-sized content. Its algorithmic approach to content discovery ensures that even users with a modest following can achieve virality, making it an attractive space for emerging creators.

Unique Features and Opportunities:

TikTok's emphasis on short, engaging videos encourages creativity and spontaneity. The 'For You' page algorithm enhances discoverability, offering creators a chance to reach a broader audience quickly. TikTok's Duet and Stitch features facilitate collaboration, fostering a sense of community among users. While TikTok does not have built-in monetization features like some other platforms, influencers often leverage brand partnerships, sponsorships, and cross-promotions to generate income.

4. Twitter

Twitter, known for its real-time microblogging format, attracts a diverse audience spanning various age groups. It is particularly popular among professionals, journalists, and those seeking to stay updated on current events. The platform's character limit encourages concise and impactful communication.

Unique Features and Opportunities:

Twitter's emphasis on brevity makes it ideal for quick updates, trends, and conversations.

Hashtags facilitate content discoverability, and retweets amplify content reach. For individuals, Twitter provides a platform to establish thought leadership, connect with like-minded individuals, and participate in broader discussions. Brand partnerships, sponsored tweets, and affiliate marketing are avenues through which users can monetize their Twitter presence.

5. LinkedIn

LinkedIn is the professional networking hub, predominantly used by individuals for career development, business networking, and industry discussions. Its user base consists of professionals, job seekers, and businesses across various sectors.

Unique Features and Opportunities:

LinkedIn's focus on professional connections makes it a valuable platform for personal branding and networking. Users can share articles, insights, and updates to position themselves as industry experts. Opportunities for income generation include job opportunities, consulting gigs, and partnerships. LinkedIn's robust search algorithm ensures that relevant content reaches a targeted professional audience.

6. Pinterest

User Demographics:

Pinterest caters to users seeking inspiration, with a predominantly female user base. It is a visual discovery platform where users curate and share ideas related to lifestyle, fashion, home decor, and more.

Unique Features and Opportunities:

Pinterest's unique feature is its focus on visual bookmarking. Users can discover content through pins, boards, and searches. Content creators, particularly in the realms of DIY, fashion, and lifestyle, can leverage Pinterest to drive traffic to blogs and websites. Affiliate marketing through product pins and collaborations with brands are potential income streams.

7. Snapchat

Snapchat is known for its ephemeral content, appealing primarily to a younger audience. Its user base consists mainly of teenagers and young adults.

Unique Features and Opportunities:

Snapchat's Stories and filters encourage creativity and spontaneous content creation. While it may not have extensive built-in monetization options, influencers on Snapchat often leverage brand partnerships, sponsored content, and exclusive access content to generate income.

Understanding the dynamics of these platforms is essential for individuals looking to diversify their online presence and explore opportunities beyond the more mainstream platforms. Each platform offers a unique space for content creation, community building, and income generation, catering to different interests and demographics.

BUILDING A PERSONAL BRAND

In the dynamic realm of social media, building a personal brand is not merely an option but a strategic imperative for individuals seeking to make a lasting impact. A personal brand goes beyond a mere online presence; it encapsulates the essence of who you are, what you stand for, and the value you bring to your audience. In this section, I will explore the significance of a cohesive brand image and delve into strategies for creating engaging and authentic content that resonates with your audience.

Importance of a Cohesive Brand Image

A cohesive brand image forms the bedrock of a successful personal brand. It serves as the visual and conceptual identity that distinguishes you from the digital noise. Consistency across various platforms fosters recognition and trust among your audience.

Here are some tips for creating a cohesive brand image:

- **Define Your Brand Values:** Clearly articulate the values you want your brand to embody. Whether it's authenticity, creativity, or expertise, these values will guide your content and interactions.

- **Visual Consistency:** Maintain consistency in your visual elements, including profile pictures, color schemes, and typography. This creates a unified and recognizable visual identity.

- **Craft a Compelling Bio:** Your bio is often the first impression. Craft a concise and compelling bio that succinctly communicates who you are and what you bring to the table.

Here's a step-by-step process to help you craft an engaging bio:

1. Introduce Yourself Clearly:

Start with your name or a recognizable username.

Consider using emojis sparingly to add personality.

2. State Your Purpose or Passion:

Briefly mention what you do or your main interests.

Highlight your primary passion or focus.

3. Show Personality:

Inject a bit of your personality into the bio.

Use a friendly and approachable tone that aligns with your brand.

4. Highlight Achievements or Credentials:

Mention relevant accomplishments or credentials.

Keep it concise and focus on what is most impressive or impactful.

5. Include Keywords:

Use keywords related to your niche or industry.

This can improve the discoverability of your profile.

6. Add a Call to Action (CTA):

Encourage followers to take a specific action.

It could be visiting your website, checking out your latest post, or subscribing to your newsletter.

7. Share Personal Touches:

Optionally, include a personal touch or fun fact about yourself.

This can make your bio more relatable.

8. Use Line Breaks and Formatting:

Break up your bio into short, readable segments.

Use line breaks or bullet points for clarity.

9. Include a Link:

If applicable, include a link to your website, portfolio, or a specific project.

Use the link strategically to direct traffic where you want.

10. Get Feedback:

Once you've drafted your bio, get feedback from friends or colleagues.

Ensure it effectively represents you and your brand.

11. Update Regularly:

Periodically revisit and update your bio to reflect changes in your life or career.

Keep it current and aligned with your evolving brand.

12. Keep it Concise:

Aim for brevity while conveying essential information.

Long bios can be overwhelming; focus on the most impactful details.

Example Draft:

🌟 Digital Marketer & Content Creator 🚀

Passionate about helping businesses thrive online.

🏆 Featured in Forbes & AdWeek

🎙 Host of the "DigitalInsights" podcast

📍 Based in [Your Location]

🔗 [YourWebsite.com]

Let's connect and elevate our online presence together! ✨

- **Show Your Personality:** Inject your personality into your brand. Whether it's humor, sincerity, or curiosity, let your unique traits shine through in your content and interactions.

Example: Consider the Instagram profile of lifestyle influencer @JoyfulAdventurer. From the vibrant color palette to the consistent use of playful emojis, her profile radiates a sense of joy and adventure.

Strategies for Creating Engaging and Authentic Content

Creating content that captivates your audience and aligns with your brand requires a thoughtful approach. Authenticity is key, as it fosters a genuine connection with your followers. **Here are strategies and tips for crafting engaging and authentic content:**

Know Your Audience: Understand your target audience's interests, preferences, and pain points. Tailor your content to resonate with them and provide value.

Storytelling: Share personal stories that align with your brand values. Authentic storytelling humanizes your brand and fosters a deeper connection with your audience.

Visual Storytelling: Leverage the power of visuals. Use high-quality images, videos, and graphics that convey your message effectively. Consider the Instagram Stories feature for behind-the-scenes glimpses.

Consistent Tone: Maintain a consistent tone in your communication. Whether it's formal, conversational, or humorous, a consistent tone builds familiarity and reinforces your brand personality.

Engage with Your Audience: Actively engage with your audience through comments, messages, and polls. This fosters a sense of community and demonstrates your genuine interest in their input.

Example: Look at the YouTube channel of tech reviewer @TechInsider. His reviews are not only informative but delivered in a conversational and approachable style, creating a connection with viewers.

Building a personal brand is an ongoing process that evolves as you grow and adapt to your audience's needs. By focusing on a cohesive brand image and creating engaging, authentic content, you can forge a brand identity that resonates, captivates, and stands the test of time. Remember, authenticity is the foundation upon which a compelling personal brand is built.

MONETIZING CONTENT

Monetizing content is a pivotal step for individuals looking to turn their online presence into a sustainable income stream. I'll delve into various monetization methods, each with its own set of pros and cons, empowering you to make informed decisions tailored to your personal brand.

1. Sponsored Posts:

Sponsored posts involve collaborating with brands to create content that promotes their products or services in exchange for payment.

Pros:

Lucrative Opportunities: Sponsored posts can offer substantial financial rewards, especially for influencers with large and engaged audiences.

Visibility and Reach: Collaborating with well-established brands can significantly increase your reach and attract new followers.

Diversified Income: It provides a steady income source, offering stability alongside other monetization methods.

Authenticity Concerns: Striking a balance between promoting a product and maintaining authenticity can be challenging, potentially risking trust with your audience.

Dependency on Brands: Reliance on sponsored content means income can fluctuate based on brand partnerships, making it less predictable.

2. Affiliate Marketing:

Affiliate marketing involves promoting third-party products or services and earning a commission for every sale or action generated through your unique affiliate link.

Pros:

Passive Income: Once set up, affiliate links can generate income passively as long as they remain relevant and drive conversions.

Diversity of Products: You have the flexibility to choose products or services aligned with your brand, ensuring authenticity in recommendations.

Scalability: As your audience grows, the potential for affiliate income also increases.

Cons:

Variable Income: Earnings can be unpredictable, depending on your audience's response to the promoted products and their purchasing behavior.

Trust Balance: Too many affiliate promotions can erode trust if not balanced with genuine, non-commercial content.

3. Selling Products/Services:

Selling your own products or services directly to your audience can be a highly rewarding monetization strategy.

Full Control: You have complete control over the products or services you offer, ensuring they align with your brand values.

Building a Brand Ecosystem: Selling products fosters a deeper connection with your audience, creating a community around your brand.

Steady Income Stream: Once established, a successful product or service can provide a consistent income stream.

Cons:

Time and Effort: Creating, marketing, and managing products or services can be time-consuming and may require additional skills.

Initial Investment: Depending on the nature of your offerings, there may be initial costs associated with product development or service setup.

4. Memberships and Subscriptions:

Offering exclusive content, community access, or perks to subscribers or members who pay a recurring fee.

Pros:

Predictable Income: Recurring memberships provide a reliable income stream, offering financial stability.

Community Building: A membership model fosters a sense of community among your most dedicated followers.

Direct Relationship: Memberships allow for direct interaction with your most engaged audience, enhancing brand loyalty.

Content Pressure: The need to consistently deliver premium content to justify subscription fees can create pressure.

Limited Reach: Exclusive content may limit your overall audience reach, as it's accessible only to paying members.

5. Ad Revenue:

Earning income through advertisements displayed on your content platforms, typically based on views, clicks, or impressions.

Passive Income: Ad revenue can provide ongoing income as long as your content continues to attract views or engagement.

Scale with Audience: As your audience grows, so does the potential for higher ad revenue.

Low Entry Barrier: Many platforms offer ad programs that are accessible even to smaller content creators.

Cons:

Dependency on Platforms: Ad revenue is subject to platform policies and algorithm changes, impacting income stability.

User Experience Impact: Excessive ads can compromise the user experience and potentially drive away followers.

The key to successful monetization lies in a thoughtful combination of these methods, tailored to your unique brand and audience. A diversified approach not only mitigates risks associated with each method but also maximizes income potential. Strive for a balance that aligns with your brand values and resonates authentically with your audience, ensuring a sustainable and mutually beneficial monetization strategy for the long term.

GROWING YOUR AUDIENCE

In the dynamic landscape of social media, growing your audience is a pivotal step towards establishing a robust online presence. This comprehensive exploration will guide you through practical tips for increasing followers organically and delve into effective collaborations and cross-promotion strategies to amplify your reach.

Tips for Increasing Followers Organically

Consistent and Quality Content:

Tip: Deliver content consistently, ensuring it aligns with your brand and provides value to your audience.

Consistency breeds familiarity, and quality content establishes trust. Regularly share content that resonates with your audience's interests, keeping them engaged and eager for more.

Optimize Profile and Bio:

Tip: Craft a compelling profile bio with keywords relevant to your niche.

Your profile serves as the first impression. A clear and concise bio, coupled with a recognizable profile picture, increases the likelihood of attracting your target audience.

Engage with Your Community:

Tip: Actively respond to comments, messages, and participate in conversations within your niche.

Genuine engagement fosters a sense of community. Responding to comments, asking questions, and participating in discussions not only enhances your online presence but also encourages others to follow you.

Utilize Hashtags Effectively:

Tip: Research and use relevant hashtags to increase discoverability.

Hashtags categorize your content and make it searchable. Identify popular and niche-specific hashtags to broaden your reach and attract users interested in your content.

Collaborate with Your Followers:

Tip: Encourage user-generated content and feature followers on your profile.

Involving your audience in your content creation process fosters a sense of community and turns followers into active participants, amplifying your organic reach.

Collaborations and Cross-Promotion Strategies

Identify Compatible Collaborators:

Tip: Seek collaborations with individuals or brands whose audience aligns with yours. Collaborating with like-minded individuals ensures that the shared audience is likely to be interested in your content, facilitating mutual growth.

Cross-Promotion on Multiple Platforms:

Tip: Cross-promote your content on various social media platforms.

Share snippets, teasers, or links across different platforms to leverage existing audiences and attract followers who may not be active on all your social media accounts.

Host Giveaways and Contests:

Tip: Organize giveaways or contests in collaboration with other creators or brands.

Giveaways encourage audience participation and attract new followers. Collaborative giveaways can expand your reach as participants often need to follow multiple accounts.

Guest Contributions and Takeovers:

Tip: Invite influencers or experts for guest contributions or takeovers.

Guest appearances introduce your profile to a new audience. Choose collaborators whose expertise complements your content, providing additional value to your followers.

Join Collaborative Campaigns:

Tip: Participate in collaborative campaigns or challenges within your niche.

Coordinated campaigns create a collective buzz, exposing your content to a broader audience. Active participation enhances visibility and engagement.

Share Each Other's Content:

Tip: Share content from collaborators and encourage them to reciprocate.

Mutual sharing strengthens relationships within your network. It introduces your content to new audiences and builds a supportive community.

Growing your audience is a multifaceted endeavor that requires a combination of organic strategies and collaborative efforts.

By consistently delivering quality content, engaging with your community, and strategically collaborating with others, you'll not only expand your follower base but also foster a vibrant and interconnected online community around your brand. Remember, genuine connections and authentic engagement are the cornerstones of sustainable audience growth.

ANALYTICS AND DATA INSIGHTS

In the digital age, harnessing the capabilities of analytics and data insights is not just an option but a strategic necessity for individuals navigating the vast landscape of social media. This comprehensive exploration will guide you through the process of using analytics tools to understand audience behavior and empower you to leverage data for optimizing both content strategy and monetization efforts.

Understanding Audience Behavior through Analytics

Choose the Right Analytics Tools:

Tip: Select analytics tools that align with your social media platforms. Popular options include Google Analytics, Instagram Insights, YouTube Analytics, and others.

Each platform offers unique analytics features. Familiarize yourself with the tools available on the platforms you use to gather comprehensive data on audience behavior.

Identify Key Metrics:

Tip: Focus on metrics that align with your goals. For example, engagement rates, click-through rates, and follower demographics.

Metrics provide a quantitative understanding of audience interactions. By identifying key indicators, you can pinpoint strengths, weaknesses, and areas for improvement.

Track Audience Demographics:

Tip: Pay attention to demographic data such as age, location, and interests.

Understanding your audience's demographics helps tailor content to their preferences, ensuring that your message resonates with the right audience.

Analyze Content Performance:

Tip: Evaluate the performance of individual posts or content types.

By analyzing content performance, you can identify which topics, formats, or posting times resonate best with your audience, allowing you to refine your content strategy.

Monitor Audience Engagement:

Tip: Track likes, comments, shares, and other forms of engagement.

Engagement metrics reflect audience interest and interaction. Analyzing these data points provides insights into the type of content that resonates most with your followers.

Utilizing Data to Optimize Content Strategy and Monetization Efforts

Identify High-Performing Content:

Tip: Use analytics to identify top-performing content and understand what makes it successful.

Analyzing high-performing content helps you replicate successful elements and tailor future content to your audience's preferences.

Content Scheduling and Timing:

Tip: Utilize data to identify optimal posting times.

Timing can significantly impact content visibility. Use analytics to determine when your audience is most active, enhancing the chances of reaching a broader audience.

Content Diversification Strategies:

Tip: Analyze data to identify content gaps or areas for diversification.

Diversifying content based on data insights ensures that your profile remains dynamic and resonates with different aspects of your audience's interests.

Evaluate Monetization Strategies:

Tip: Use analytics to assess the effectiveness of different monetization methods.

Monitor the performance of sponsored posts, affiliate marketing, product sales, or any other revenue streams. Adjust your strategies based on which methods yield the best results.

Optimize Ad Campaigns:

Tip: If using paid advertising, continually refine and optimize based on analytics data.

Analyzing ad performance data allows you to allocate budgets effectively, target the right audience, and refine ad creatives for maximum impact.

Conversion Tracking:

Tip: Implement conversion tracking to measure the effectiveness of your monetization efforts.

Whether it's tracking product sales, affiliate link clicks, or other conversion events, understanding the conversion funnel provides valuable insights into user behavior and preferences.

Iterative Strategy Refinement:

Tip: Use analytics data as a feedback loop for continuous improvement.

Social media is dynamic. Regularly assess analytics data to refine your strategies, ensuring that you adapt to evolving audience behavior and industry trends.

Analytics and data insights empower you to make informed decisions, optimize your content strategy, and maximize monetization efforts. By embracing data-driven strategies, you not only gain a deeper understanding of your audience but also position yourself for sustained growth and success in the ever-evolving landscape of social media. Remember, the true power lies not just in collecting data but in utilizing it strategically to fuel your journey towards achieving your goals.

LEGAL AND ETHICAL CONSIDERATIONS IN NAVIGATING THE SOCIAL MEDIA LANDSCAPE

In the rapidly evolving realm of social media, creators and influencers must navigate legal and ethical considerations to build a sustainable and trustworthy online presence. This comprehensive exploration will guide you through crucial legal aspects, including copyright issues and disclosure requirements, and delve into ethical practices that are paramount for maintaining trust with your audience.

Legal Considerations

Copyright Issues:

Understanding: Respect intellectual property rights and avoid using copyrighted material without permission.

Best Practices: Create original content, obtain proper licenses for third-party content, and always credit sources appropriately.

Disclosure Requirements:

Understanding: Transparency is key when it comes to sponsored content or affiliate marketing.

Best Practices: Clearly disclose partnerships, sponsorships, or affiliate relationships to maintain transparency and comply with local regulations. Use clear and easily understandable language.

Privacy Laws:

Understanding: Respect user privacy and adhere to data protection laws.

Best Practices: Clearly communicate how user data will be used and ensure compliance with privacy laws, such as GDPR or CCPA, depending on your audience's location.

Defamation and Libel:

Understanding: Be cautious about making false statements that harm someone's reputation.

Best Practices: Fact-check information before sharing, avoid making unfounded accusations, and be aware of potential legal consequences for spreading false information.

Contest and Giveaway Compliance:

Understanding: Ensure compliance with local laws and social media platform guidelines for contests and giveaways.

Best Practices: Clearly outline rules, eligibility criteria, and prize details. Adhere to platform-specific guidelines to avoid penalties or account restrictions.

Ethical Practices for Maintaining Audience Trust:

Authenticity and Transparency:

Guideline: Be genuine and transparent about your content, partnerships, and experiences.

Best Practices: Clearly communicate your values, motivations, and experiences. Avoid deceptive practices that could undermine trust with your audience.

User Consent and Respect:

Guideline: Obtain user consent before using or featuring their content.

Best Practices: Respect user privacy and seek permission before using user-generated content. Give credit where due and engage with your audience in a respectful manner.

Avoid Deceptive Marketing Practices:

Guideline: Do not engage in deceptive tactics to boost engagement or inflate metrics.

Best Practices: Avoid clickbait, misleading titles, or manipulative tactics. Provide accurate information to your audience to build trust over the long term.

Community Engagement:

Guideline: Foster a positive and inclusive community.

Best Practices: Moderate your platforms to create a safe space for your audience.

Encourage respectful discussions and address any inappropriate behavior promptly.

Responsible Influencer Marketing:

Guideline: Evaluate the impact and ethics of products or services you promote.

Best Practices: Align with brands and products that align with your values and are genuinely beneficial to your audience. Avoid promoting harmful or misleading products.

Avoiding Plagiarism and Proper Attribution:

Guideline: Respect intellectual property and give proper credit.

Best Practices: Create original content and attribute sources appropriately when using third-party content. Avoid using others' work without permission or proper credit.

In the dynamic world of social media, legal and ethical considerations are foundational pillars that sustain your credibility and longevity as a content creator. By understanding and adhering to copyright laws, disclosure requirements, and ethical practices, you not only protect yourself legally but also foster a relationship of trust with your audience. Remember, ethical behavior isn't just a legal necessity; it's the cornerstone of building a community that values authenticity, transparency, and mutual respect.

DIVERSIFYING INCOME STREAMS

In the ever-changing landscape of social media, diversifying income streams is a strategic move that not only enhances financial stability but also safeguards against uncertainties. This comprehensive exploration will guide you through various additional revenue streams beyond social media, emphasizing the importance of a diversified approach for long-term sustainability.

Beyond Social Media: Exploring Additional Revenue Streams

Online Courses and Educational Content:

Opportunity: Create and sell online courses, webinars, or educational content.

Benefits: Leverage your expertise to provide value, and capitalize on a growing demand for online learning. Platforms like Udemy, Teachable, or your own website can be utilized.

Merchandise and E-commerce:

Opportunity: Design and sell branded merchandise related to your content.

Benefits: Merchandise such as apparel, accessories, or digital products can serve as an extension of your brand. Platforms like Shopify, Printful, or Teespring facilitate easy integration with your social media presence.

Affiliate Marketing Beyond Social Media:

Opportunity: Expand affiliate marketing efforts to blogs or email newsletters.

Benefits: Beyond social media, affiliate marketing can be integrated into other online channels, providing an additional income stream through product recommendations and reviews.

Consulting or Coaching Services:

Opportunity: Offer personalized consulting or coaching services.

Benefits: Utilize your expertise to provide one-on-one guidance. Platforms like Clarity.fm or private consulting sessions can be avenues for monetizing your knowledge and skills.

Public Speaking Engagements:

Opportunity: Explore opportunities for public speaking engagements or workshops.

Benefits: Speaking at conferences, events, or webinars can not only provide monetary compensation but also enhance your industry authority and visibility.

Writing and Content Creation for Others:

Opportunity: Provide freelance writing or content creation services.

Benefits: Expand your skills to cater to businesses or publications. Platforms like Upwork or freelancing websites can connect you with potential clients.

Embracing a Diversified Approach for Long-Term Sustainability

Risk Mitigation:

Strategy: Diversifying income streams spreads risk across various channels.

Rationale: Relying solely on social media platforms for income can be risky due to algorithm changes or unexpected disruptions. A diversified approach ensures that income is not solely dependent on a single source.

Audience Expansion:

Strategy: Explore new platforms and mediums to reach a broader audience.

Rationale: Diversification involves expanding your presence to platforms beyond social media. Podcasts, blogs, or emerging platforms can attract new audiences and diversify your income potential.

Adaptability to Market Trends:

Strategy: Stay abreast of industry trends and adapt your offerings accordingly.

Rationale: Markets evolve, and diversified income streams allow you to pivot when necessary. Be open to exploring emerging trends and adjusting your approach to meet changing demands.

Resilience in Economic Downturns:

Strategy: Ensure that income streams are not solely reliant on discretionary spending.

Rationale: Economic downturns can impact consumer spending on certain products or services. A diversified income portfolio may include recession-resistant streams, providing stability during economic uncertainties.

Leveraging Existing Skills:

Strategy: Identify and leverage skills beyond content creation.

Rationale: Your skills extend beyond creating content. Whether it's teaching, consulting, or providing services, diversification allows you to capitalize on a broader skill set.

Building a Sustainable Brand Ecosystem:

Strategy: Integrate income streams into a cohesive brand ecosystem.

Rationale: Ensure that additional revenue streams align with your brand identity. A cohesive brand ecosystem creates synergies between different income channels, reinforcing your overall brand presence.

Diversifying income streams is not just a financial strategy; it's a proactive step toward building a resilient and sustainable online presence. By exploring opportunities beyond social media, adapting to market trends, and leveraging a diverse skill set, you not only safeguard your financial future but also enhance your ability to adapt and thrive in the ever-evolving landscape of digital entrepreneurship. Remember, the key to long-term success lies in embracing diversity, both in income streams and the strategies you employ to nurture your online brand.

OVERCOMING CHALLENGES IN THE SOCIAL MEDIA LANDSCAPE

In the dynamic realm of social media, creators often encounter a myriad of challenges, from algorithm changes to facing negativity. Navigating these hurdles requires not only resilience but also a proactive approach to adapt to the ever-evolving landscape. This in-depth exploration will address common challenges and share effective strategies for overcoming them.

Algorithm Changes:

Challenge:

Social media platforms frequently update their algorithms, impacting content visibility.

Strategies for Overcoming:

- **Diversify Content Formats:** Create diverse content types to align with potential algorithm shifts.

- **Stay Informed:** Keep abreast of algorithm updates and adjust your content strategy accordingly.

- **Engage Authentically:** Genuine engagement can mitigate the impact of algorithm changes by fostering a loyal audience.

Dealing with Negativity:

Challenge:

Negative comments, criticism, or online harassment can impact mental well-being.

Strategies for Overcoming:

- **Focus on Positivity**: Emphasize positive content to counterbalance negativity.

- **Moderate Effectively:** Establish clear community guidelines and moderate comments proactively.

- **Seek Support:** Reach out to friends, peers, or mental health professionals for support during challenging times.

Follower Fluctuations:

Challenge:

Fluctuations in follower count can be disheartening.

Strategies for Overcoming:

- **Focus on Engagement:** Prioritize meaningful engagement over raw follower numbers.

- **Audit and Refine**: Periodically review and refine your content strategy to attract and retain followers.

- **Set Realistic Expectations**: Understand that follower counts can fluctuate; consistency and quality matter more than rapid growth.

Content Saturation:

Challenge:

Oversaturation of content in a specific niche can impact discoverability.

Strategies for Overcoming:

- **Niche Refinement:** Refine your niche to cater to a more specific audience.

- **Collaborate and Network:** Collaborate with other creators to tap into different audiences.

- **Quality Over Quantity:** Emphasize high-quality content that stands out amid saturation.

Evolving Trends:

Challenge:

Keeping up with rapidly changing trends can be challenging.

Strategies for Overcoming:

- **Continuous Learning:** Stay informed about industry trends through courses, conferences, and networking.

- **Experimentation**: Embrace experimentation to identify what resonates with your audience amid evolving trends.

- **Collaborative Learning:** Engage with other creators to share insights and stay collectively aware of emerging trends.

Privacy Concerns:

Challenge:

Increasing awareness of privacy issues can impact user trust.

Strategies for Overcoming:

- **Transparent Practices:** Clearly communicate your data practices to your audience.

- **Compliance:** Stay informed about and adhere to privacy laws and platform policies.

- **Secure Communication:** Use secure channels for communication and transactions to protect user privacy.

Platform Dependence:

Challenge:

Relying solely on a single platform for income or audience engagement poses risks.

Strategies for Overcoming:

- **Diversify Income Streams:** Explore additional revenue streams beyond the primary platform.

- **Cross-Platform Presence:** Establish a presence on multiple platforms to mitigate risks associated with platform dependence.

- **Own Your Content:** Create and promote content on platforms you have more control over, such as a personal website or newsletter.

Coping with Burnout:

Challenge:

The pressure to consistently produce content can lead to burnout.

Strategies for Overcoming:

- **Set Boundaries**: Establish clear boundaries for work hours and personal time.

- **Prioritize Well-being:** Regularly check in on your mental and physical health.

- **Delegate Tasks:** Consider delegating certain tasks or seeking assistance to alleviate workload pressures.

Overcoming challenges in the social media landscape requires a combination of resilience, adaptability, and proactive strategies. By acknowledging the ever-changing nature of the digital space, creators can navigate algorithm changes, negativity, and other hurdles effectively. Embrace a mindset of continuous learning, engage with your community authentically, and diversify both your content and income streams to build a robust and sustainable online presence. Remember, the ability to overcome challenges not only strengthens your personal brand but also positions you as a dynamic and resilient force in the evolving world of social media.

SUCCESS STORIES AND CASE STUDIES

In the vast landscape of social media, success stories and case studies illuminate the paths of individuals who transformed their online presence into thriving monetization ventures. This exploration delves into real-life examples, extracting key lessons from their journeys, offering insights for those seeking to embark on a similar path.

1. Case Study: PewDiePie (Felix Kjellberg)

Background:

Platform: YouTube

Monetization Methods: Ad revenue, sponsorships, merchandise, book deals, and brand partnerships.

Key Lessons:

1. Authenticity Wins: PewDiePie's genuine personality and unfiltered content played a pivotal role in attracting a massive audience.

2. Diversify Income Streams: Beyond ad revenue, he successfully diversified by exploring merchandise sales, brand partnerships, and even a book deal, showcasing the power of multiple revenue channels.

3. Adapt to Changes: PewDiePie constantly adapts to evolving trends, keeping his content fresh and appealing to a broad audience.

2. Case Study: Huda Kattan (Huda Beauty)

Background:

Platform: Instagram, YouTube, and a personal beauty blog

Monetization Methods: Beauty products, collaborations, affiliate marketing, and sponsored content.

Key Lessons:

1. Building a Brand Ecosystem: Huda Beauty seamlessly integrates her social

media presence with a successful cosmetics line, creating a cohesive brand ecosystem.

2. Engage and Educate: Regularly engaging with her audience, Huda provides valuable beauty tips and tutorials, establishing herself as an expert and cultivating trust.

3. Diversify Beyond Social Media: The brand's expansion into the beauty industry exemplifies the potential for creators to extend their influence beyond social media platforms.

3. Case Study: Tim Ferriss

Background:

Platform: Blog, Podcast, and various social media platforms

Monetization Methods: Bestselling books, podcast sponsorships, public speaking engagements, and online courses.

Key Lessons:

1. Content Repurposing: Tim Ferriss adeptly repurposes content across multiple mediums, from blog posts to podcasts, maximizing reach and impact.

2. Leverage Expertise: Through best-selling books and online courses,

Ferriss leverages his expertise to create valuable products and services.

3. Strategic Partnerships: Successful podcast sponsorships demonstrate the potential for strategic partnerships to enhance revenue streams.

4. Case Study: Chiara Ferragni (The Blonde Salad)

Background:

Platform: Fashion and lifestyle blog, Instagram

Monetization Methods: Fashion collaborations, endorsements, brand partnerships, and her own fashion line.

Key Lessons:

1. Influence as a Business: Chiara Ferragni transformed her fashion blog into a full-fledged business, exemplifying the potential for influencers to become entrepreneurs.

2. Brand Collaborations: Successful collaborations with major fashion brands showcase the lucrative opportunities for influencers to monetize their influence.

3. Brand Extension: Ferragni successfully extended her brand with a fashion line,

illustrating the power of diversification in revenue streams.

5. Case Study: Pat Flynn (Smart Passive Income)

Background:

Platform: Blog, Podcast, YouTube

Monetization Methods: Affiliate marketing, online courses, book sales, speaking engagements, and podcast sponsorships.

Key Lessons:

Transparent Income Reports: Pat Flynn's transparency in sharing income reports has built trust with his audience, showcasing the potential for authenticity in content creation.

Education as a Revenue Stream: Through online courses and books, Flynn monetizes his expertise, illustrating the value of educational content.

Diversify with Integrity: Flynn's approach to affiliate marketing focuses on recommending products genuinely used and trusted, emphasizing the importance of ethical monetization.

These success stories and case studies illustrate that the journey to monetizing a social media presence is diverse, requiring creativity, adaptability, and a strategic mindset. The key lessons extracted include the importance of authenticity, the power of diversifying income streams, and the potential for creators to become entrepreneurs. Whether it's leveraging expertise, building a brand ecosystem, or strategically collaborating, these case studies offer valuable insights for those aspiring to turn their social media presence into a successful and sustainable venture. Remember, success is not a one-size-fits-all formula; it's a personalized journey fueled by passion, innovation, and a commitment to delivering value to your audience.

FUTURE TRENDS AND ADAPTATION IN SOCIAL MEDIA

As we stand at the cusp of the future, the dynamic landscape of social media continues to shape-shift, presenting creators and influencers with new challenges and opportunities. This exploration delves into emerging trends in social media and provides insights on staying ahead of the curve, emphasizing the importance of continuous learning and adaptation.

Emerging Trends in Social Media

Short-Form Video Dominance

Trend: Platforms like TikTok and Instagram Reels are witnessing a surge in popularity, emphasizing short-form, engaging video content.

Adaptation: Creators should explore concise storytelling and creative expression within the short-form video format.

Virtual and Augmented Reality Integration:

Trend: VR and AR technologies are becoming more accessible, offering immersive experiences for users.

Adaptation: Creators can explore interactive content, virtual events, or even augmented reality filters to enhance user engagement.

Niche Communities and Micro-Influencers

Trend: Niche-focused platforms are gaining traction, and micro-influencers are proving to have a more significant impact within specific communities.

Adaptation: Creators should consider niching down their content to cater to specific interests and building genuine connections within smaller, engaged communities.

Ephemeral Content and Disappearing Stories

Trend: Platforms like Snapchat and Instagram Stories have popularized ephemeral content.

Adaptation: Creators can leverage the urgency of disappearing content to create a sense of exclusivity and immediacy, driving engagement.

Social Commerce Evolution

Trend: Social media platforms are increasingly integrating shopping features, creating a seamless shopping experience.

Adaptation: Creators can explore partnerships with brands, utilize in-app shopping tools, and create content that seamlessly integrates product recommendations.

Staying Ahead of the Curve

Continuous Learning and Skill Development

Strategy: Embrace a mindset of continuous learning to stay informed about emerging trends and technologies.

Rationale: Regularly participate in courses, webinars, or industry conferences to expand your skill set and stay ahead of the ever-evolving social media landscape.

Experimentation and Risk-Taking

Strategy: Be willing to experiment with new content formats, platforms, or technologies.

Rationale: Innovation often stems from taking calculated risks. Embracing experimentation allows creators to discover what resonates with their audience and adapt accordingly.

Community Engagement and Feedback

Strategy: Foster active engagement with your audience and seek feedback on your content.

Rationale: Your audience is a valuable source of insights. Engage in conversations, conduct polls, and use feedback to tailor your content to evolving preferences.

Cross-Platform Presence

Strategy: Establish a presence on multiple platforms to diversify your reach.

Rationale: Platforms evolve, and emerging trends may gain prominence on different channels. Diversifying your presence ensures adaptability to shifting trends and audience behaviors.

Data Analysis and Insights Utilization

Strategy: Leverage analytics tools to analyze audience behavior and content performance.

Rationale: Data-driven insights provide valuable information on what works and what doesn't. Use analytics to refine your content strategy and adapt to changing audience preferences.

Networking and Collaboration

Strategy: Build connections within the social media and influencer community.

Rationale: Networking allows you to exchange insights, collaborate on projects, and stay informed about industry trends. Collaborations also introduce you to new audiences.

Agility and Adaptability

Strategy: Develop an agile mindset and be ready to pivot when necessary.

Rationale: The digital landscape is dynamic. Creators who adapt quickly to emerging trends and changes can seize opportunities and maintain relevance.

As I envision the future of social media, embracing change becomes not just a necessity but a strategic imperative. By understanding emerging trends, actively engaging with your audience, and continuously evolving your skills, you position yourself not just as an observer but as a proactive participant in the shaping of the digital landscape. The creators who flourish in the future are those who can adeptly adapt, innovate, and ride the waves of change with resilience and creativity. Remember, the future belongs to those who stay curious, learn relentlessly, and fearlessly embrace the unfolding opportunities within the ever-evolving social media ecosystem.

CONCLUSION

As I conclude this comprehensive exploration into the world of social media monetization, let's distill the key takeaways that can serve as a compass for your journey and inspire you to embark on this exciting venture.

1. Diverse Revenue Streams Are Key:

Takeaway: Success in social media monetization lies in diversifying your income streams. Explore avenues beyond ad revenue, such as sponsored content, affiliate marketing, merchandise sales, and online courses.

Inspiration: Embrace the versatility of monetization opportunities, transforming your social media presence into a multifaceted revenue-generating engine.

2. Building a Cohesive Brand Is Essential:
Takeaway: A strong, cohesive brand image is the foundation of successful monetization. Focus on authenticity, engage with your audience, and ensure that your content aligns with your brand identity.

Inspiration: Your brand is your unique fingerprint in the digital landscape. Craft it with care, and let it resonate authentically with your audience.

3. Continuous Learning and Adaptation Are Imperative:

Takeaway: The social media landscape is ever-evolving. Stay ahead of the curve by continuously learning about emerging trends, experimenting with new formats, and adapting to changes.

Inspiration: The journey of social media monetization is a dynamic one. Embrace the thrill of staying agile and learning, evolving not just with the trends but ahead of them.

4. Trust and Transparency Build Long-Lasting Connections:

Takeaway: Building trust with your audience through transparent practices is invaluable. Disclose partnerships, respect privacy, and maintain ethical practices to cultivate a loyal and engaged following.

Inspiration: Trust is the currency of social media. Upholding transparency and ethical standards not only safeguards your brand but also strengthens the bond with your audience.

5. Passion Fuels Resilience:

Takeaway: Passion for your content and your audience is the driving force behind resilience. Stay true to your interests, create content that excites you, and let your enthusiasm shine through.

Inspiration: The passion you infuse into your content becomes the magnetic force that attracts and sustains your audience. Let it be the beacon guiding your journey.

6. Adapt to the Future:

Takeaway: Anticipate and adapt to future trends in social media. From short-form videos to virtual reality, the landscape is ever-expanding. Embrace change with curiosity and an open mind.

Inspiration: The future of social media holds limitless possibilities. Be a pioneer, experiment with emerging trends, and shape the landscape rather than merely following its trajectory.

In the vast realm of social media monetization, you are not just a spectator; you are a protagonist crafting your narrative. Seize the key takeaways as your tools, use them to sculpt your unique brand, and embark on a journey where creativity meets commerce. The canvas of social media awaits your strokes, and the potential for financial growth and creative fulfillment is boundless.

So, whether you're a seasoned creator seeking new horizons or a budding influencer ready to unfold your story, step into the world of social media monetization with purpose, passion, and an unwavering commitment to your unique voice. The digital stage is yours, and the possibilities are as expansive as your imagination. Let the journey begin, and may your story be etched in the vibrant tapestry of social media success.

www.ingramcontent.com/pod-product-compliance
Lightning Source LLC
LaVergne TN
LVHW051657050326
832903LV00032B/3868